SOUTH ISLAND TINY HOUSE

OUR JOURNEY MOVING TO NEW ZEALAND AND
BUILDING A TINY HOUSE ON WHEELS.

CORIANNE HOLMES

Dedicated to Gloria F. Holmes and my family

1
WHY DID WE GO TINY?

 "Every great dream begins with a dreamer."

—HARRIET TUBMAN

*Patrick and Cori standing on the tiny house deck on their
property in Dunedin, New Zealand.*

WE ARE PATRICK AND CORI, two average American millennials living in New Zealand. When we were young twentysomethings, we just wanted a home and a good life, but we knew we had to get creative to get it. We met in Boston when I (Cori) was twenty-two. I was a new graduate of Wellesley College and was working at my first full-time job. Patrick was twenty-six, a small business owner, and a full-time employee. At the time he was living with his twin brother in Manchester, New Hampshire.

Patrick and I both grew up middle class with hard-working, loving parents and a few siblings between us. I grew up in the Midwest and Pat on the East Coast. We enjoy the outdoors and love music, movies, and projects. But more than anything our relationship bloomed and thrived with our love of sharing and investigating ideas with one another. Patrick is my rock, my sounding board, my biggest cheerleader, and my knight in shining armor. I am his helper, voice of reason, motivational speaker, and emotional support.

The South Island Tiny House would not have been possible if we hadn't worked as a team and brought our various skills, roles, and quirks to the table. And as with many strong relationships, building something together not only seemed possible but almost necessary. Sometimes the urge to create tangible proof of your partnership is too strong to ignore. And although we didn't know it at the time, our casual conversations about small living would actually pan out.

So, really, the story of the South Island Tiny House begins with our relationship. The first time I went to Patrick's house, I knew I had nabbed a winner. It was spotless, well organized, and clean, and he pointed out all the things he had made, fixed, or installed in his house. When we went down to the garage, I knew this was a handy dude. So naturally, I immediately put him to work. Kidding! He kindly offered to help me with maintaining my Prius, he painted my condo while I was traveling, he built me extra storage in my bathroom, and he fixed things I was happy to just "deal" with. I felt like I had struck gold. I found myself daydreaming about the projects he could build for me. It was truly novel having someone so handy and capable at my beck and call.

When I saw beautiful shipping container homes online, I knew Pat would be interested. What ambitious welder with unmatched diligence toward large projects wouldn't be interested? And he was! Even though we are both big dreamers, we understood the realities of our circumstances. It was a pipe dream, but we sustained ourselves with research and YouTube.

Pat and Cori stopping in Malibu as they drove down US Route 101 to LA before flying to New Zealand in 2014.

It didn't take us long to discover the tiny house movement. It seemed to be within the same vein as shipping container homes but without needing land first. We were excited by the variety of tiny houses that people had made (which was fairly limited back in 2012) and the potential savings on rent. At the time we were paying for two places, and since we spent every free moment together anyway, it seemed extremely wasteful and expensive to us. Small living seemed so perfect for our circumstances.

Small spaces didn't scare us; we found them fascinating! Pat told me about his childhood treehouse in the forest behind the old Toys"R"Us building near the Manchester Mall. Pat, his twin, and their crew of friends built it themselves using tools stolen from his dad's workshop. They pieced it together with free scraps they found behind the huge chain stores nearby and spent most of their free time after school in their private domain. I told him about the odd architectural features around my childhood home where my sister and I would hide, build blanket forts, and have puppet shows. Both our childhoods were spent in and out of doors enjoying small places, so naturally we felt like living in a small place would be easy for us.

As we contemplated the challenges of our living situations, we began to ask the big questions about where we wanted to live and whether the United States was even the right place for us. Did we really want to live in a tiny house during a harsh winter? We made a pros and cons list and started ranking and eliminating locations. The United States didn't make the cut. New Zealand topped the list, simply because it was the easiest country for us to move to. I was already a permanent resident of New Zealand thanks to my parents' initiative when I was twelve. I knew it well, had a bank account there, and could get my master's degree for much cheaper than in the States. So, once I was accepted into the University of Canterbury for a one-year Master of Business Management program, everything fell into place.

In order to finance the move, we decided we needed at least $20,000 in New Zealand dollars ($15,400 US dollars) to comfortably start a new life in New Zealand. We contributed equally to a high-interest savings account, and after selling items we couldn't take with us, we quickly and easily got to our number after a few months. We purchased our tickets and Patrick secured his visa, and before we knew it, we were in Christchurch, New Zealand.

I was familiar with Christchurch before the 2011 earthquake struck, but I didn't really consider the situation beyond the earthquake's destruction. I had no idea that the price of rentals would be affected by the aftermath of the earthquake. We quickly learned that the majority of the housing stock in the city was either destroyed or in the process of being repaired. We had just picked up and dumped our lives into an expensive and competitive foreign real estate market. What a wake-up call! When we first arrived, we stayed with friends. Then after going to multiple viewings, we secured a room in a four-bedroom flat. It was cramped and on a busy road. There was one bathroom and laundry room for six adults and our room could barely fit a bed, let alone a desk. After a few weeks of misery, a flat at the university opened up. It was moldy, lacked insulation, and was horribly outdated, but at least we didn't have to share it.

Our experience with these two rentals showed us all we needed to know about New Zealand's subpar housing. It was especially shocking because we had both spent our entire lives in warm, cozy, well-built homes in the United States. Neither of us had an interest in living that way for long. But what could we do? We couldn't afford much better.

Pat and Cori on the beach in 2018.

Coming to this realization wasn't simple or obvious to us at the time. We both struggled to adjust to our new life and eventually came to the same conclusion—we were broke and miserable. Sure, we could have used "moving to New Zealand" money to rent a better flat, but then we would have completely depleted our life savings. And we wouldn't have been able to stay in the nice flat forever, as our income wasn't high enough. Our relationship took a hit during this time. Our social lives were nonexistent in Christchurch during that first year, and we missed the variety and nightlife of Boston. I was busy with school and my two, sometimes three, part-time jobs, and Pat struggled to keep himself busy after work. We shared an old Honda, which limited our independence from each other. Our lives couldn't have been more different from when we first started dating. As we dealt with the disappointments of having our grand visions of a life in New Zealand dissolve into reality, we remembered the tiny house movement. Revisiting those tiny dreams helped us through our first year living in New Zealand.

During the Christmas holidays of 2014, we decided to use our "moving to New Zealand" money for a tiny house. Luckily, we had barely touched the money because Pat had secured a job as soon as we arrived. After we made our decision, it took two months for Pat to find the perfect trailer for us on Trade Me (a popular online auction and classifieds website in New Zealand). The owner was unable to use it for his own tiny house build because of an ended relationship. We jumped at the opportunity mostly because the $3,000 in New Zealand dollars ($2,310 US dollars) price was the lowest we had seen. After agreeing to the purchase, we scrambled to find a place to build the tiny house because our small flat didn't have a yard to speak of. Luckily, thanks to another purchase on Trade Me, we found a kind llama farmer who had an available paddock that we rented for $150 New Zealand dollars ($115 US dollars) per month. Once the trailer was acquired and delivered to the llama paddock in Rolleston, about twenty minutes from the moldy flat in Christchurch, the real work began.

2
REBELS WITH A CAUSE

 "What is a rebel? A man who says no."

—ALBERT CAMUS

Tiny house in Rolleston, Canterbury, New Zealand.

WHEN WE BEGAN RESEARCHING tiny houses in New Zealand, we knew the movement thrived in a certain legal sweet spot. Based on our research, as long as a tiny house *can* be *legally* moved and *is* moved often enough, it can't be considered as a fixed and permanently occupied structure. This means a tiny house must be a road-legal structure, and one must prove that it is by relocating every so often. But then again, the law is open to a bit of interpretation—for instance, how fixed is fixed? How long can someone live somewhere before it is considered to be permanently occupied? We were willing to accept these uncertainties because we were only going to spend $20,000 New Zealand dollars ($15,400 US dollars) on the whole build, and we weren't planning on living in the tiny house forever. So, although it made sense for us, tiny house living is not a solution for every situation.

———

IN NEW ZEALAND, there have been two recent legal decisions about tiny houses; both have reinforced our original thoughts and opinions about the tiny house movement. We were correct in thinking that the movement operates in a gray area and that if you push the rules too far, there are consequences.

The first decision is from the Environment Court of New Zealand. In *Fadi Antoun v Hutt City Council* [2020] NZEnvC 6, Fadi claimed that the two-story tiny house he had built on steel beams was a vehicle and that the Resource Management Act 1991 couldn't be applied in his situation.

Let's look at the facts. The structure Fadi built had two axles (that weren't even connected), and the wheels were separate from the structure. These were the only two obvious indications that he was attempting to build a tiny house; everything else pointed to "permanent structure."

The judge was not at all convinced that Fadi had built a tiny house on wheels and stated as much in his determination. He found "the contention that the tiny house is a vehicle to be a flight of imagination advanced to justify the failure to apply for any necessary resource consents to construct it."

These were the points the court made while explaining why the tiny house was subject to the law under the Resource Management Act 1991:

- The look and design indicated that it was fit to be used for permanent occupation.

- There were plans in place to connect the tiny house to services.

- The tiny house was built on the ground (not on the trailer) and was supported by steel beams.

- The tiny house could not be converted into a trailer or loaded onto a vehicle (because it was too big).

The court determined that Fadi's tiny house had to comply with the Resource Management Act 1991 and the rules of the district plan. This seems like an obvious case to me, as does the second case, *Dall v MBIE* [2020] NZDC 2612.

This case involves Mr. Dall, who constructed a road-legal tiny house on a warranted and registered trailer. Unfortunately, some grumpy neighbors complained about his setup. He asked the Ministry of Business, Innovation and Employment to decide if his tiny house should be considered a "building," in terms of section 8 of the Building Act 2004; a "vehicle"; or a "motor vehicle." Mr. Dall felt confident that his tiny house did not apply to the regulations in the act (as shown in the following image).

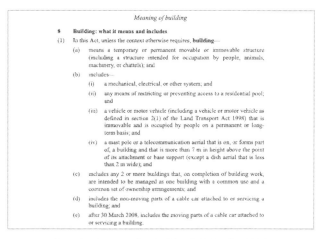

Snapshot from section 8 of the Building Act 2004.

Surprisingly, MBIE concluded that the tiny house was in fact a building and that the council was justified in going after his tiny house. Mr. Dall immediately appealed to the District Court.

The District Court rightly focused on the two required legal aspects for a vehicle to be considered as a de facto building. The first is that the vehicle is immovable; the second is that it is occupied by people on a permanent basis. Mr. Dall was obviously occupying the space on a permanent basis, but he wanted the court to recognize that his tiny house was movable.

The court went down the rabbit hole of technicalities. It said that technically every house is movable. Look at transportable houses or houses that are built in factories or off-site from a build and then craned or transported to another site. If one uses this reasoning, no house in New Zealand would have to be built under the Building Act 2004, because every house can technically be moved. And that would frankly be ludicrous. So the court focused instead on the degree to which it is practical to move a structure. To determine this, the court looked into Mr. Dall's tiny house's design, the function of its various characteristics, and the ultimate purpose of the tiny house.

Mr. Dall's tiny house has all the hallmarks of a vehicle: wheels, brakes, axles, lights, drawbar, and trailer hitch. These aspects of the tiny house were functional, and the ultimate purpose for them was so that the house could be moved. Eventually, the court agreed with Mr. Dall and held that the tiny house was not immovable because it was on a registered and warranted trailer that had all the requirements to be road legal.

Mr. Dall was very pleased with this outcome, I am sure, but the court also included something in its determination that lots of people on tiny house Facebook pages have continually brought up and even done, which is to build a tiny house that can be removed from the trailer. The court clearly stated at the end of this case that it would have come to a different conclusion if the tiny house had been designed so that it could be moved off the wheels and fixed to the land. So hopefully those people online are aware of this warning!

It's hard not to feel smug about doing your own research, making a calculated decision, and then being validated by the legal system. But I do feel a tiny bit bad for those people who took it too far. When building a tiny house, you must build it to minimum building standards. It's not a free-for-all. You can't build it out of popsicle sticks and hot glue and expect it to stay in one piece as you move it from one place to another. And you can't build a house and essentially draw on wheels and say "Voilà! A tiny house!" There are parameters and rules, believe it or not, within which you have to build. However, that being said, Pat and I agreed early on that if we were ever contacted by a local council because a grouchy neighbor or ornery passerby decided to complain, and were given a notice to fix, we would demonstrate our tiny house's design and function by hooking it up and driving it the hell away.

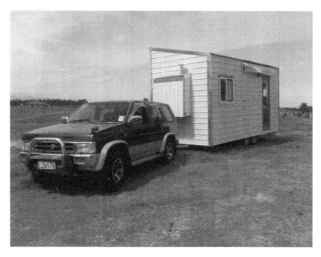

Our first time towing the tiny house.

3
DECISIONS, DECISIONS, DECISIONS

 "You just have to believe in your decisions, and keep one eye towards your goals."

—ARBER DOCI

TURNS OUT, getting the trailer for the tiny house was the easiest part of our tiny house journey. As the designated project manager and boss of the build, Patrick had his work cut out for him. I left all research into the legal requirements for trailer sizes to him. While I did my homework in the evening, Patrick scoured the Internet for information on how to build a tiny house and thought through the important decisions we needed to make before we started building. Our first step was to design the tiny house, and this involved a remarkable amount of chalk.

According to the New Zealand Transportation Agency trailer specifications, the legal dimensions for a light trailer are 12.5 meters (41 feet) long, including a tow bar; 2.55 meters (8 feet, 4 3/8 inches) wide; and 4.3 meters (14 feet, 1 1/4 inches) high, including the load. The total weight can't exceed 3,500 kilograms (7,716.179 lb.). With this knowledge and our already-built trailer measuring 6.2 meters (20 feet, 8 inches) long and 2.4 meters (7 feet, 10 inches) wide, we had our limitations clearly defined. And with that, we began bingeing tiny house content, constantly latching on to ideas and designs, sketching and redesigning our dream tiny house in our heads and on paper. We were most inspired by the Minim tiny house design in terms of the placement for the bed. However, because our trailer was so small, putting the bed under the floor didn't leave many options for the kitchen and bathroom. We weren't too bothered by those limitations however, and we were able to incorporate everything we wanted into our final design, including a loft, just not for sleeping.

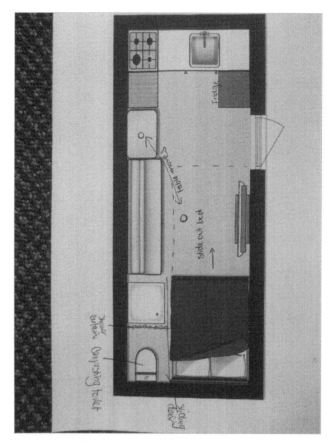

Early mock-up of the tiny house design.

As we considered adding a loft to our design, we were struck by how generous the legal height for a trailer seemed. We thought of all the downsides of having a tall, tiny house:

- We would need to buy a very tall ladder.
- The finished tiny house would be more dangerous to transport.
- Taller tiny house equals more materials.
- How would we get into the loft? Ladder? Staircase? That means less floor space.
- The loft would add to the total weight of the tiny house.
- If we added a chimney flue, the total height could put us over the legal road limit.

- Heating and cooling is difficult for a loft. Would we get overheated sleeping up there?

These scared us so much that in the end, we settled for a small storage loft instead. This was the first of many design compromises we made while building. It comes with the territory of having such a small budget. We knew we would never be able to build the *ultimate* Truly Luxurious Tiny House. We saw some beautiful tiny homes with marble countertops, huge bathtubs, washer-dryer units, massive fridges, two couches, spare bedrooms, and so on. These items are not only expensive, but they are also heavy. And this touches on the second thing that scared us. Above all, we wanted to stay within our budget and within our weight limit. And since one of the reasons for building a tiny house was that we didn't want to stay in Christchurch forever, we knew that at some point the tiny house would need to be on the highway. The more we thought about it, the more we realized that having a loft would never trump the possibility of ending up with a tiny house that we couldn't move.

The other important reason we wanted to stay underweight was towing. It is extremely nerve-racking to take one's tiny house on the road. There is a lot at risk, and building an overweight tiny house won't make the move (or subsequent moves) any easier. The average tow hitch of a heavy-duty vehicle is rated for the legal limits of a trailer. It is important to build to these parameters, otherwise you risk damaging the vehicle and tow hitch. Another important consideration was balancing our tiny house. We needed to design and build the tiny house (and place the items inside) so that the weight was distributed over the axles safely. Tongue weight is also an important consideration. If the trailer's tongue is too light, the trailer can swerve, but if there is too much weight, it can affect the tow hitch and vehicle suspension. Typically, nine to fifteen percent of the total weight of the tiny house should be on the tongue of the trailer.

An example of a small-sized trailer suitable for a tiny house.

Most tiny houses are built on two or three axles, and depending on the number you have, this will also affect the total weight the trailer can handle. Ours only has two axles. There are also the trailer wheels to consider. How much weight could the wheels on our trailer handle? Not a lot. We did a rough estimation of our final design weight to see if it was feasible. In this we calculated the building materials, our personal items, the trailer itself, the axles, the wheels, the trailer tow hitch, the trailer tow bar, our vehicle, the vehicle's tow bar, and the vehicle's tow hitch.

We were pretty sure that we could build our tiny house under the legal weight limit, but we had to plan for the worst-case scenario, just in case. At the time all we owned was the tiny house trailer and a Honda Accord. So we laid out our options for getting the tiny house from point A to B, assuming our house was the legal weight and size, and determined we could:

- Buy an average truck to tow the tiny house.
- Borrow or rent a truck to tow the house.
- Hire a company to tow the house.

These were all realistic options for us, but what scared us were our options if the tiny house was over the legal weight. We could:

- Buy a big, expensive truck and get a new license to be able to tow an overweight vehicle.
- Search high and low for a company that would tow an overweight tiny house—they would either refuse or charge a huge amount for insurance.
- Tow our tiny house with our license and average truck anyway and have our house break, the trailer hitch break, or end up breaking the law if we got pulled over.

So with those terrifying potentials haunting our dreams, we embarked on our tiny house build. And although we didn't buy an industrial scale to weigh everything we put on the trailer, we were *extremely* thoughtful and aware of everything we used in the build. And in the end, we kept the tiny house underweight and purchased an average truck to tow it. We believed it to be the simplest, cheapest, and easiest option.

4

STICKING TO THE BUDGET

 "We must consult our means rather than our wishes."

—GEORGE WASHINGTON

ONCE PATRICK and I weighed up our options, we agreed that the legal risk was worth taking and settled on the ideal size and weight of our tiny house. Afterwards, we moved on to gathering materials. Patrick has always been a curious sort, always asking around at work if something was destined for the skip. He also possesses the unique talent of being able to immediately assess whether something is worth saving. So while Patrick was slowly collecting discarded items from the construction sites where he was working, we started sourcing other used building materials such as windows and doors. We searched for items that were cheap, light, and in good condition. It was a real challenge finding lightweight materials, as a lot of the housing materials available were heavy since the weight of building materials doesn't affect much in a typical house.

In our case, we discovered that the cladding we'd selected could provide the same level of stability as plywood. This was a welcome discovery, as plywood is expensive in New Zealand!

When we began collecting tools, general building materials, and various items for the tiny house, we pretty much got whatever we thought "might" work. It didn't take long for our small flat to become a dump. We found ourselves with a huge stockpile of free materials from construction sites, some newly purchased materials, secondhand goods, general building tools, and recycled items. Without all of these free materials, our tiny house budget would have been completely blown!

Once the build got underway, we were very glad to have the majority of our materials ready and available. However, it was only at the final moment of installation that we would realize an item just wouldn't fit. Although it was easy collecting, we had to be very efficient with eliminating surplus materials that didn't work.

Below are some examples of items that just didn't work. We tried hard not to let our vision and reality fight each other for too long. Reality usually won out in the end. This was abundantly clear when we stopped to consider our tight budget and limited time frame. We needed to finish the tiny house before the lease on our flat ran out.

Example 1: I desperately wanted these recycled lockers to act as our pantry in the kitchen. But the dimensions and space just didn't work out. Since we had already squeezed them into our Honda Accord and brought them all the way out to the tiny house, we wanted to incorporate them into the house design somewhere! We decided to use the lockers as our closet near our bathroom. They were so heavy that it was a relief to finally set them down after we had made our decision.

Interior of the tiny house with the lockers at the back, which served as our closet for a few months.

Example 2: We bought some beautiful used parquet wood flooring from Trade Me. But when it was time to install the flooring, we realized that we would need a lot more materials to properly install it.

And most importantly, it would take skills we didn't have—and didn't have time to learn! So we sold the floor, bought some laminate flooring, and installed it over the course of a weekend. Much easier and quicker. Not as nice, no, but time was of the essence.

Our new laminate flooring, which Pat installed in a few hours
—much faster than parquet!

Example 3: We purchased a brand-new four-burner stovetop for the kitchen from Trade Me, but as soon as we got it out of the box and placed it on the countertop, we knew that we would lose too much counter space. So we sold it and bought a smaller two-burner stovetop that fit perfectly.

The kitchen counters we thought were big enough for a four-burner stovetop.

The two-burner stovetop we ended up installing in the kitchen.

Example 4: We found an old suitcase that we imagined would make a great "medicine cabinet" for the bathroom. Yet when we held it up to the wall, it was clear there was no way it would fit. So I came up with the idea of using it to hide the plumbing under the sink. And I discovered there was still a bit of room for my collection of essential oils!

Example 5: We knew we wanted something comfy for the sitting area in the house and thought, *what is comfier than a nice couch?* We got a used brown couch to save on the budget, modified it a bit, and were frankly horrified with how it looked in the space. It was awkward, too

big, and just plain ugly. So we brought it home and chucked it out. We would have saved time by just burning the $150 New Zealand dollars ($115 US dollars) we spent on it! So instead we used leftover plywood, mattress foam, and stapled fabric over the whole thing. And we ended up sitting on it for five years!

The cushioning on our homemade couch.

It didn't take long for us to realize how important it is to think on our feet, assess the viability of an idea quickly, and not be afraid to think creatively. Most importantly, these examples illustrate that there is no shame in cutting your losses and moving on to plan B. Thank god we never succumbed to indecisiveness—we would have never finished otherwise!

5
PUTTING IN THE WORK

 "Without labor, nothing prospers."

—SOPHOCLES

A llama check-in on our progress.

AS THE DAUNTING task of building a house loomed, we added to our stress by starting a tiny house blog. We viewed the blog as an accountability tool, but it eventually became an annoying afterthought as the construction ramped up. (See for yourself at www.southislandtinyhouse.wordpress.com; it peters out quite suddenly.)

We decided early in the build that the best way to stick to our $20,000 New Zealand dollar ($15,400 US dollar) budget was to track our purchases. Luckily, a lot of our materials were free, but we still ended up with a lot of receipts! Obviously, purchases on Trade Me didn't come with receipts, so it was a bit more difficult to keep track of those. Saving receipts saved us in a few situations where we had purchased expensive tools from Bunnings (a local hardware store); when they broke, simply because we kept the receipts, we were able to replace the tools fairly easily. Additionally, when it came time for Patrick to prove his intention on staying in New Zealand for his permanent residency application, these receipts showed the immigration officer his commitment to living in New Zealand.

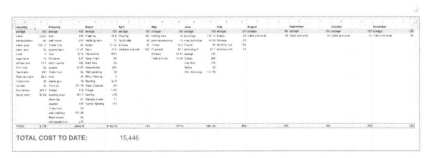

We got lazy near the end of the build when we didn't need many materials but just needed to install the items. We also didn't track the solar panel system, but it came in at around $5,000.

Trade Me was by far the most frustrating source for building materials and appliances, but it was also the best source for variety and price. I suppose the reason we had so many annoying encounters with sellers and buyers was due to the sheer volume of transactions we were involved in for over a year. All in all, we didn't have much choice with sources for materials; Christchurch has limited options. In addition to tracking purchases, we also found that having one account with all the money for the build helped us to keep close track of the cost.

Our first task on the tiny house build was to get the trailer in good enough condition to start building. Like a foundation for a house, the trailer for a tiny house on wheels is very important. Our trailer came with some railings and some rusty spots. Patrick used his grinder to cut off the railing, and we used a rust converter product to prepare the trailer before painting it with rust-proof paint. Once the trailer was ready, we considered our next steps.

Simply screwing some plywood onto the trailer for our floor was never going to cut it for us. Insulation was a necessity for temperature consistency. We were not interested in sharing our tiny house with bugs or mice, so a thick barrier between the inside and outside was a must. The tiny house also needed a sturdy floor that wouldn't warp over time, as it needed to keep its integrity on the road. Lastly, we wanted to avoid dampness that would cause mold or rot.

So, with our requirements in mind, we built the frame for the floor and attached some leftover vinyl to act as a moisture, bug, and mold barrier. Once that was completed, we fixed it to the trailer. We then used ceiling insulation and foam inside the cavities and topped the whole thing with multiple layers of plywood. The floor was officially done!

*Cori enjoying the sun after finishing the first major component
of the tiny house build.*

It was at this point that the weather stopped cooperating. As if by design, it promptly rained as soon as we secured the first thing on the tiny house that we didn't want to get wet—the plywood floor. We rushed to purchase tarps from Bunnings and tried to tie them to the trailer, but we soon learned that attaching tarps to a trailer in the middle of a windy paddock and hoping it would stay put all week was extremely naive. (We were always surprised on Saturday mornings to see what kind of damage the previous week had brought to our tiny house build.) Luckily, everything dried out adequately before we began framing.

The windows and doors had already been purchased early on from Brown Sparrow (a used window and door business in Christchurch), and it was very helpful having them at the building site. The downside of having glass windows and doors in a paddock was that the llamas in said paddock had zero respect for these expensive purchases that were lying in the grass. A large llama footprint made of mud, poo, and hay mocked us by surviving on the front door (yes, even after it was installed) for over five months before we remembered to bring window cleaner with us one Saturday morning.

The windows and front door in the llama paddock.

The framing went together with little fanfare; however, some unforeseen situations took place immediately afterward. First, the walls were much taller than we expected. And we only had one ladder at the time. We had no choice but to soldier on. There was quite a bit of swearing, yelling, and straining to get them in place. And on top of these struggles, one wall was almost secured to the trailer before we realized it was upside down. Another wall's window had been built without consideration for the elevated portion of our floor. By the time we recognized this second mistake, we accepted our fate. We were just going to have to live with an awkwardly placed window at "junk height" near the bathroom.

We started the build after the longest day of the year, and we felt the pinch of time every weekend as we found our daylight hours shortening. But it really started to matter after the framing was completed. Instead of hot, sunny days, we were then wrangling tarps, dealing with waterlogged timber, and freezing as the sun dipped below the horizon.

We knew that our next objective should be to get the house watertight so we could at least have access to some sort of shelter as we worked. This would also provide a safe, dry place for the building materials we were transferring from the flat to the paddock. Patrick single-handedly added the roof to our tiny house over the course of a weekend while I was busy with work and school. We decided on a mono-pitch roof because of the ease of installation and the fact that it would maximize the internal space in the tiny house. The roof only required a few sheets of used corrugated iron. Pat even laid the sheets so that the existing holes lined up, thus eliminating the need for loads of silicone sealant to prevent leaks. The roof also helped to stiffen up the walls on the tiny house, which was reassuring after we'd watched the entire build wrapped up in tarps catch the Canterbury wind several times.

The cheapest building paper that Bunnings had for sale at the time was this brand of black wax paper that could only be left exposed for three weeks. So from the moment we stapled the paper to our timber, we were under a lot of time pressure. Opting to forgo the typical plywood exterior before installing the cladding not only kept the weight down on the trailer but also made the process faster and cheaper. Pat insisted on nailing the cladding (one of the few items we bought new) in a certain pattern. From sunup to sundown on one chilly Saturday, Pat straddled the only ladder we owned, and I passed him nails and fetched the hammer after he threw it into the middle of the paddock in frustration. After just a few weekends, the cladding was up. The windows and doors followed, and before we knew it, our house was watertight! It was such a relief that day to be able to keep our compressor, generator, ladder, and other tools inside our tiny house (all the wood went under the house). We locked the door and went home with a huge sense of accomplishment.

This elation only lasted as long as it took for us to understand just how much work was left to make the tiny house habitable. The next logical step was running the electrical wiring along the walls and deciding on the location of outlets and light switches. The plumbing followed next in our order of execution, and it was here that we started to comprehend some of the space-related challenges involved in building a tiny house. Not only did we need to shift the tools, ladders, materials, and other miscellaneous items from corner to corner and side to side of the house depending on where we were working but also, we kept realizing that before some new task could be completed, we'd need to install something else first. We were more or less constantly rearranging our to-do list, rescheduling purchases, and putting things on hold. On top of this, there were often delays because we were dependent on Pat being able to bring certain tools home from his jobsite.

Some easy projects included the flooring, as the laminate was going to be placed throughout the tiny house. It was straightforward to install and then cover it with protective plastic so that we could continue working without worrying about damaging the floor. The loft space was another easy project as it had no plugs, plumbing, or lighting. Other relatively simple tasks included the reclaimed wood statement wall (the wood needed to be cut and nailed to the wall) and the crates (we outsourced these items and all we needed to do was cut them to fit over the wheel wells). The more challenging projects included the kitchen (which involved lighting, plugs, gas, water, and plumbing), the raised floor (we needed to hide the bathroom plumbing, gas lines, electric wiring, and we had to fit the bed underneath), and the bathroom (we were running out of materials by that point).

The first order of business, once we embarked on the interior of the tiny house, was the loft above the kitchen. It was surprisingly easy and finishing the loft space early in the build was extremely helpful. Once it was up, we could start bringing our stored materials to the tiny house that we had been hoarding at our moldy flat. All the free insulation Patrick had secured was stuffed into about eight trash bags and luckily all eight bags fit in the loft, allowing us to keep it dry and out of the way.

The statement wall was a breeze once we got into the rhythm of things. We insulated the whole wall first, and then the process was simple: pick a piece of wood, trim off the bad part, wipe off the bird shit, grab the brad nail gun, *boom boom boom*, NEXT!

Then we installed the flooring, which was a breeze after I informed Pat that he was doing it in the wrong direction. It took several days to finish. Luckily, Patrick sourced some leftover floor protection from his current job, so we were able to cover the laminate and protect the floor while we continued the build.

Then we brought in the kitchen cabinet. This item was so annoying to carry, move, and shift, which inevitably meant we were obliged to move it in and out of place no less than four times. The kitchen had the wood statement wall on one side, and we decided to use some leftover cladding for the other two sides until we arrived at the door. We finished up the exposed parts with used lauan (thin wood) and cut up recycled crates that we got from a friend. The counter was completed shortly thereafter, thanks to Pat's backyard welding (he completed our U-shaped stainless steel counter on two completely different-sized grills), and the gas and plugs were in place. So at this point we had a kitchen, a statement wall, a loft, and a floor.

Next up was the raised floor, which was mostly Pat's job. When I joined him one Saturday afternoon, he informed me that the second floor was much better than the first. Did I mention that we were building without any drawings or schematics? If you choose to wing it as we did, mistakes will be made, and when you become aware that something won't work, the best way to deal with it is to try again, but quickly because daylight is a limited resource. After the raised floor was completed and laminate flooring installed on top, we were ready to put together our bed frame and slats that Pat had brought all the way from the United States (on the plane) to the tiny house. This went together easily, as we had calculated it down to the millimeter.

As we progressed, we realized we hadn't decided what we wanted to use for the rest of the interior cladding. We liked the look of the kitchen, and the statement wall was amazing, so we just figured, why not continue the theme of "cheap and lazy" throughout the rest of the house? After the insulation had been stuffed into every nook and cranny, the rest of the external metal cladding went up inside the tiny house; we tackled the ceiling immediately afterward because our arms didn't hurt enough after holding heavy sheets of corrugated iron, picking up dropped screws, and balancing on two mismatched ladders for what seemed like hours. It was exhausting.

At this point, we were halfway through the build. We should have felt proud of our progress and confident in completing the build, but sometimes just arriving at the tiny house would lead to a complete mental breakdown. There was so much left to do; everywhere we looked all we saw were tasks that still needed to be done. In hindsight, we were fortunate to build our tiny house away from our flat because it gave us the necessary space to plan the rest of the build without getting overwhelmed (too much).

Our solution to these woes was to tackle a number of small tasks at every visit and to put all the problems that we didn't have solutions for to the side. So with that new strategy in mind, we installed the crates that had been recently delivered and we cut them to size and installed them. But we didn't have any clue how to make them into a comfy bench, so we benched that problem.

The bed came together fairly quickly. It was a simple matter of following the Ikea instructions, using some leftover wood from the build, and attaching appliance wheels. We didn't know where we were going to put our pillows, though, so we put that problem to the side.

The bathroom was the last large task we needed to tackle. But it was a fast job because we didn't have to wait for much of anything—it was all ready to go. We framed the walls first, secured the cladding, installed the shower, attached the sink to the wall, and hooked up the plumbing. We easily solved the small problem of what to do with the ceiling (we were down to our *last* two sheets of white metal cladding) by adding a strip of wood to bridge the gap. We used cheap fifty-cent stick-on tiles for the floor and built a sliding door. We were undecided on what type of toilet to purchase or build, so we put that problem to the side.

The final touches on the tiny house included adding built-in storage around the house, building the TV area, trimming the windows (outside and inside), installing the solar panels, and completing general improvements as we came across issues or solutions to make living tiny more comfortable. But what really made our tiny house feel like home was moving our things into the new space and decorating it to suit our style.

So it was almost anticlimactic once the tiny house was finally "done." In fact, it was nerve-racking knowing that we were going to be moving in shortly. We still had our lease at the moldy flat for a few more months, and it was getting annoying having to keep some kitchen items at the flat when we wanted to install them in the tiny house. We made sure everything was running and working before we suggested to my mother that she stay in the tiny house while she visited for my graduation from the University of Canterbury. She was ecstatic with the idea. It was great to have someone else approve of our build, ideas, and design.

6

TINY HOUSE LIFE AND TRIALS

 "A lot of hard work is hidden behind nice things."

—RALPH LAUREN

WHEN THE TINY house was nearing completion, we asked the llama farmer if she was interested in renting a small corner of her least-used paddock to us full time. As we suspected, she wasn't. So we commenced Operation Find Some Land.

We told everyone we knew—friends, work colleagues, and acquaintances. We posted propositions on Facebook and even looked into buying land. One day, we pulled over on the side of the road and asked someone if he had plans with his empty lot. The man looked like he was planning on shooting us as we said "hi" and tried to shake his hand, so we didn't try that approach again. But we thought we should take advantage of all the cheap sections available in Christchurch at the time. After weeks of searching, we eventually found an absolute minuscule section close to the central business district of Christchurch that we thought might work for us.

We met the owner after a few weeks of emailing back and forth. Unfortunately, it had also been a few long weeks of rain. When we finally arrived, we were shocked that the section appeared to be 100 percent mud. I remember standing there in our raincoats in shock at just how small the section was at about fifty square meters (0.01 of an acre). The lot would barely have enough room for the tiny house, a small deck, and maybe a vehicle. At least there was a nice fence around it. But the opening, we decided, was the biggest impediment. We didn't think we could even get the tiny house through the opening.

We went home to have a long, hard think about the section. We could take down the fence and replace it (expensive) or crane the tiny house over the fence into the section (expensive) or try to wedge it through the opening (expensive if the tiny house got damaged). In the end, however, the decision was out of our hands because a few weeks later the Christchurch City Council made a new rule effectively banning tiny houses (structures under ten square meters or 107.39 square feet) from the central business district, so that was that.

With the end in sight, we always figured our plan B could be just rolling up to a trailer park or campsite and paying nightly for a little while until we found something more permanent. But as luck would have it, the llama farmer had spoken about us with her neighbor and he was interested in meeting. Patrick met with him, and they hit it off right away.

The couple who owned the land were already renting out a cottage on their property, so they had experience with unique situations, and they had land to spare. Since their property was next door to the llama farm, it was a very "simple" procedure to relocate the tiny house. You might be thinking, *how convenient for you!* It was bittersweet because we had *just* purchased a heavy-duty vehicle capable of towing our tiny house, anticipating a much longer and more involved move, but it turned out that there was no need for it because our new landlord owned a tractor! But to be fair, the truck we had purchased was handy for hauling materials during the build, so I suppose we got our money's worth.

With our future rental worries assuaged and as the house became more and more complete, we were eager to see how the tiny house would tow. One day we decided to do a practice run moving the tiny house around the llama paddock with the truck. It was immediately obvious that the truck was barely able to handle the tiny house (which was completely empty at this point!), so thank goodness we didn't need to use the truck to move it.

We decided to finish the solar panel system and wood burner once the tiny house was in a more permanent location. In October, the fateful day arrived, and we were ready and waiting with butterflies in our stomachs. We had packed up all of our tools the day before; all we needed to do was hook the tiny house up to our new landlord's tractor and follow behind in our truck. We even asked if one of our friends could help with traffic management. But it wasn't necessary. It took all of five minutes to leave the paddock and then about one minute on the main road before turning down the next long driveway to another paddock, which would become our home. Though it wasn't a long process, the whole time Pat and I were barely breathing. It was so nerve-racking, following behind our beloved tiny house that we had only known as a stationary object!

When the tractor passed through the gate to our small paddock, curious and slightly alarmed sheep looked on. The paddock was fairly flat already, so minimal work was needed to make it livable. Our new landlord was kind enough to dig a deep hole for our gray water with his tractor. We needed water to the house as well and decided the cheapest solution was to run a hose over from the main house and connect it to the tiny house. In exchange for the small piece of land and water, we paid the couple $100 New Zealand dollars ($77 US dollars) a week.

Wasting no time, Pat spent the next weekend working on the porch. He was able to get some unused plywood walls from the Christchurch Art Gallery, where he was working, and turned them into our temporary porch floor. The *very* next day a blind sheep got stuck under the porch and couldn't get out! Poor Patrick had to crawl under the house, through sheep poop, and grab its legs to help it out. We built a fence later that day. During this time we still had our moldy flat, but we had most of our things in the tiny house. We spent a lot of time going back and forth, unsure of when our official move-in date should be. Luckily, some alums from my alma mater, Wellesley College, contacted me; they were traveling in the area and looking for a place to crash. We decided to let them stay in the flat and we officially moved into the tiny house. It was sublime!

We spent a considerable amount of time making the tiny house as cozy as possible. We had room for my car, Pat's work van, and the truck we initially brought to move the tiny house. Our porch was soon covered with plants, an outdoor seating area, a barbecue grill, and a washer. We had everything we needed. It was cozy and fun spending our first summer in the tiny house.

———

 "Expect problems and eat them for breakfast."

—ALFRED A. MONTAPERT

EVERYTHING WAS GOING great with our lives in the tiny house until it wasn't. The excitement of finally living in the tiny house was awesome that first summer, especially over the holidays. But after about three months of working at my new job, I was feeling unsatisfied and unfulfilled; I slowly grasped that it was actually a step backward in terms of earnings compared to what I was making in the United States and on top of that I was paying off the loans for my master's program. We were lucky that our expenses were much lower than the average person, but we began to register how wasteful we were being in certain ways.

After spending our savings on the tiny house, we needed to rethink our budget. The first thing that had to go was the truck, which was no longer serving a purpose. It was fun to have when we went down to the local river, we could drive through the water, no problem. But the truck wasn't necessary. Once we sold it and no longer had to pay for the upkeep and petrol, losing this extra expense gave us a huge sense of relief. We also began to sell some of the larger, more expensive tools we had purchased to build the tiny house. Selling the truck and the tools helped a bit but didn't affect our expenses.

We were paying off a loan for my master's degree, establishing an emergency savings account, saving for our future, and contributing to our KiwiSaver (a New Zealand-based voluntary retirement fund). Then, in the midst of a massive saving mode, I began to travel for work. Although I appreciated the work, we were feeling a bit burned-out from all the constant disruption to our lives.

As summer came to an end, some issues started to appear with our tiny house setup. One night the compressor on the fridge, which we had come to be very familiar with as it was a bit noisy, kept starting and stopping—so often that it woke us up. We figured the fridge was broken, so we tried to make do with a cooler while we sent the fridge to Auckland to get it fixed under its warranty. The company sent it back and it worked for a bit, but eventually the problem returned. So we bought another type of fridge altogether.

This time we purchased a three-way fridge. A three-way fridge can be run with 240V, 12V, or with liquefied petroleum gas (propane in the US). So we ran it with LPG for a few weeks but the fridge we had purchased wasn't the best. It was used and didn't have the same capacity as our old one. It took a few weeks of us being unhappy before we figured out that we should have considered the batteries as being the source of the first fridge's issues.

We monitored the batteries over the next few days. They always seemed extremely low, even after a full day of sun. So we talked to a local battery expert; he said one of our batteries was toast and that the other was working twice as hard and as a result had gone bad as well. We were stunned that our brand-new batteries had gone bad so quickly. The batteries weren't covered by any sort of warranty. We were so disappointed we had wasted our money buying a defective battery.

The local battery guy lent us some large batteries until we were able to order new ones (from a more reputable company). We were so grateful to get the loaner batteries because as soon as we had removed the defective batteries for testing, we couldn't run anything in the house. Thank god the shower ran off of the on-demand hot water heater. While we were waiting, we decided to get another solar panel to make doubly sure that charging wasn't the issue.

All in all, it took about two months to figure out the root of our problems, but boy was that a stressful time. We burned candles, purchased ice every day for our food that we stored in a cooler, spent time on the phone with various businesses, and wasted many a night furiously Googling what could be wrong with our house (the wiring? the solar panels? the batteries? the fridge? the inverter? our usage?).

We had no instructions for our new life, neither for our tiny house nor its systems. We had to figure everything out ourselves. So after all that, we decided to buy *another* fridge, just a normal bar fridge that used about the same wattage as the "special" solar fridge that alerted us to the problem in the first place. So there we were with three fridges, an additional solar panel, and a general fear of using too much electricity, all while dealing with a lot of travel. Both Patrick and I were frequently out of town. Tiny house drama plus our busy personal lives caused some serious burn out. We seriously thought maybe this tiny house idea was a complete fail. But we pushed through the doubts and started plotting because the way we were living was unsustainable.

Things were also changing around us, the one-year marker for me being at my job was coming up and I had to stay the course to avoid having to pay back my signing bonus. The Christchurch rebuild was also starting to slow down with many anchor projects beginning and the end was in sight. As a result, Pat was assigned to a job out of town and started to travel out of town every day. Simultaneously, his company was trying to plan and organize an upcoming project in Glenavy, a small town between Waimate and Oamaru. They would need someone to live closer to the work site and gave Pat the option to move and the company would pay for a rental. We knew the project wouldn't last forever so understood that we needed to have a plan for where we were going to go afterwards. But we were excited by the possibilities, namely moving further south to Dunedin! We both felt the time was right, so he agreed, and we knew it was time to leave Christchurch and take our tiny house south!

7

A FORK IN THE ROAD

 "The first step towards getting somewhere is to decide you're not going to stay where you are."

— JP MORGAN

AS OUR LUCK would have it, as soon as I stopped traveling for work, Patrick's work gave him two options for his next project, Queenstown or Ashburton. He chose Ashburton and committed to a long, boring daily commute. Four months of all that driving and he had just about had it. Once he finished with the project in Ashburton, he had a slightly different perspective when his work gave him another choice for his next project: Glenavy or Queenstown. We chose Glenavy, but since it was so far from Christchurch, this meant moving the tiny house and living there. His work was extremely generous in paying for our accommodation, and because of that, I decided to leave my job and take a break from working.

Glenavy was a bit too small (no available rentals), so we decided that Waimate would be our home base and Pat would commute the twenty minutes. We were excited and very nervous to move to such a rural town in New Zealand. I was most nervous about making a good impression on the locals. Mostly, though, I didn't want any mobs chasing us out of town because we showed up in the middle of the night and parked our tiny house in the driveway of the accommodation provided by Patrick's work. Many hours went into preparing for the move and there was a lot of stress involved. There was a lot to do before we could move.

In order to tackle it all, step by step, we made a list of everything that needed to be done, then organized it by date on the calendar. This is just a short list of what we needed to do:

1. Clean up our setup (porch, shed, fence, plants, etc.)
2. Secure transportation for the house (we didn't own a vehicle that could tow the tiny house)
3. Weigh the tiny house (so if we were pulled over we could produce evidence that we were under the limit)
4. Find a place to park the tiny house and live
5. Make sure the neighbors (and the general community) didn't hate us
6. Move the tiny house, pack up the car, and pack up the cat

We began by cleaning out the shed we had near the house (the landlord was kind enough to let us use it). This was mostly full of tools from the build and wood that we had purchased for burning in the winter. We then, sadly, had to get rid of our garden. The only plant we took with us was my lemon tree. We packed up the washer and some of the other items we were storing on the deck. Once that was done, we cleared off the deck and dismantled it and the porch. Unfortunately for us, it rained that night. Turns out our deck was protecting not only the porch but also the door. So we were very surprised when we woke up to a wet floor and water seeping into the house! After a quick trip to Spotlight (a fabric and haberdashery store), we found a heavy-duty plastic door covering that we put up when it was due to rain to keep our door from leaking. Ah, the joys of secondhand doors!

With the porch gone, we only had a few wooden steps to get into the tiny house, and although it was annoying, at least the tiny house was ready to be moved. Next, we started looking for a way to transport the tiny house to Waimate. Patrick asked his project manager if he could swap work vehicles for a few days. But to make sure the borrowed truck could handle the task, we hooked the tiny house up to it for a test run the day before we were due to leave. We decided to kill two birds with one stone and not only tested the truck but also slowly drove down to the weigh station, which luckily was only minutes from the farm. Finally knowing the weight of our tiny house after almost a year of living in it was really gratifying. We had taken so much care to build it with the final weight in mind, so we were elated to find that our cautious building yielded us a tiny house that only weighed 2.4 tons. This meant we didn't have to worry about the combined vehicle and load weight or getting a fine while transporting the tiny house to Waimate.

We happily returned to the paddock with the tiny house and went looking for our cat, who was out wandering while we were away. We discovered, upon her return, that she had a pretty bad open wound on her side. We rushed her to the vet to get her fixed up. The vet cleaned the wound, stapled the sides together, and fitted her with a cone. We were under strict instructions to keep her movements to a minimum so she wouldn't tear the staple out. On top of that, we couldn't feed her dinner, because she had a habit of pooping in her carrier while traveling in the car. So we had an uncomfortable and unhappy cat that was stuck inside the tiny house with us as we tried our best to rest before leaving the paddock in the early hours of the morning.

It was really hard being in the tiny house that night because it wasn't hooked up to anything. The water hose had been disconnected and we had no power because the batteries had been put away. I kept going over to the sink to get water, opening the tap and forgetting that there was no water! We didn't sleep a wink from worrying about the cat, stressing about towing the house to Waimate, and worrying about leaving Christchurch. Poor Meow Meows was in a cone, with a wound that a few hours after returning from the vet had ripped open again, and she kept reminding us that she was absolutely starving (we try not to feed the cat before taking her in the car as she has a tendency of going to the bathroom in her crate while in the car)!

Pat and I lay on the bed, side-by-side in our clothes, for a few hours before gave up trying to sleep and just decided to just leave at 1:30 a.m. instead of waiting until 3:00. We took everything down from the shelves in the kitchen and over the TV, laid the heavy items (like our books) flat in the shower, and took all of our items off hooks. After getting the tiny house situated, I got the cat into the carrier and got into my car. The plan was for me to follow Pat, who was driving the truck towing the tiny house. It was a calm and chilly night. I was shaking the entire time from nerves; the cat could probably tell because she howled and yowled the entire time. She didn't even let up when I called Patrick to let him know the tiny house was swaying a little and that he should slow down. All in all, the trip took about four hours and we only hit top speeds of sixty kilometers per hour or about thirty-seven miles an hour. It was the longest four hours of my life.

———

AS WE PULLED INTO WAIMATE, the sun was already up but everything was still quiet. Before our move south, I posted a Facebook message on the Waimate community page to see if anyone would be interested in a tiny house tour. I figured, why not get everyone's curiosity out of their systems all at once while the tiny house was still mobile and in a convenient spot? I did not think this idea through. So as soon as we pulled into town, we parked the tiny house, unpacked a little bit to make it look normal again, and dropped the cat off at the rental house (we locked her in a small sunroom so she wouldn't get lost or reinjure herself). At this point, we were absolutely exhausted, but we had an open house to host!

We got our lawn chairs and sat outside our tiny house for about three hours as more than two hundred people walked through the house. Some had seen the Facebook ad; others were just passing through. The Waimate Community Market was on at the same time, so that brought in additional numbers. It was a great time. We got to meet some locals and show off our hard work, and it helped us adjust to the idea of living in a typical rural, small town in New Zealand.

After the open house, we moved the tiny house to the driveway of the rental for which Pat's work was paying. We backed it into the driveway, connected the water and gray water, and that was it. We were done! Well, I was done; Patrick still had to drive back to Christchurch to return the truck and get his van back. But he returned the next day, and then we could finally rest. Before everything closed for the Christmas holiday, we had a chance to get Meow Meows looked at by another vet, explore the wonderful hikes Waimate has to offer, and enjoy our holiday! My Facebook post garnered lots of attention and we had a few articles written about us in the *Daily Mail*, Stuff (an online news website: Stuff.co.nz) and the *Timaru Courier* (New Zealand). I was over the moon! And to top off 2016, Pat proposed on New Year's Eve and everything in our lives was going swimmingly.

Then shit hit the fan.

8
TINY HOUSE ON THE RUN

 "If you can meet with Triumph and Disaster

And treat those two impostors just the same."

—RUDYARD KIPLING

WE LIVED BLISSFULLY in our tiny house that summer in Waimate, making friends, going to the beach, hiking, volunteering at the Waimate Community Garden, and basking in our newly engaged status. During that holiday we enjoyed ourselves but we were also busy setting up our next steps.

If there is one thing we learned from living in a tiny house, it is to always have plans percolating in the background. In our discussions about our long-term plans and dreams, Dunedin had always been mentioned. So we decided this was the time to finally start taking steps to move to our dream town.

Luckily, Pat knew a former work colleague who had worked for a company in Dunedin before relocating to Christchurch, where they met. He recommended Pat to his old boss and Pat easily got his foot in the door. It took two trips down to Dunedin from Waimate for him to have a job offer in hand, so thankfully his employment in Dunedin was all settled. He was scheduled to begin on April 1, 2017. That left us with our tiny house to sort.

We looked at a few lots in the area (north and south of Dunedin), but we were having a hard time finding land to rent. Then we remembered that one year prior (when we were still in Christchurch), my parents had planned to build a house in Waitati, a suburb of Dunedin, but my parents ultimately decided against having a house built while at a distance. This fortuitous situation had me thinking. Maybe we could put our tiny house on the vacant lot until they decided what they wanted to do with it! It took a few months of convincing and cajoling, but eventually, we felt sure that we had a place for the tiny house.

It seemed like the perfect solution for us to move the tiny house there in order to begin clearing the property of the overgrown weeds and to bring power and water back to the section and make it useful again. But these plans were fluid at the time. Soon a threat of losing the tiny house would change things.

The first time we looked at the property, we were stunned. It needed a lot of work to get it ready for a tiny house, let alone a big house! All we could see was a driveway and a small shed. Everything else was covered in weeds and trees. We tried to scope out what we could access, but the grass and weeds were very overgrown. We had our work cut out for us.

The first few trips to the property we were just getting our heads around it, to see what really needed to be accomplished. Pat decided that the most efficient way to level the property was to rent a machine and then he would run the piping for water. So we began the next weekend after we found a place to rent a Bobcat machine.

The most affordable option was in Timaru. We left Waimate early on Saturday during the Christmas holiday, drove north to Timaru, and then grabbed the trailer with the Bobcat from the owner's house. We then proceeded south past Waimate and headed to the property. About halfway we had a blowout on the trailer tire.

I was in a full panic. When we could stop safely, we attempted to call AA (which is the New Zealand version of AAA). But there wasn't a single AA-affiliated garage nearby. Luckily, I remembered seeing a sign for a garage a few miles behind us, so we took a chance and limped the trailer there. They were able to fix the tire and we were soon back on the road. We started to worry the whole trip was going to be a waste, as time was running short considering all the work that had to be done. We only had the Bobcat for the day, plus we still had to drive back to Timaru to return it.

So after getting the trailer back on the road, we finally arrived at the property and unloaded the machine. Pat got to work right away, pushing and leveling the mound of dirt and weeds that were sitting exactly where we wanted to put the tiny house. After a few hours of hard work, mostly staying out of the way for my part, I noticed that the track on the Bobcat was coming off the rim. I got Patrick's attention and he stopped just in time. He was able to maneuver the track back into place. Instead of trying to tempt fate once more with our horrible luck, we decided to call it a day. We brought the trailer and Bobcat back to Timaru and then headed home. After one crazy eventful day, the property was flat!

We ended up heading to the property just about every weekend as there was so much to do. We had to run the piping, get the gravel delivered, and set up our mail. The most expensive was the electricity, which involved digging a deep trench, running the electrical conduit, installing a builder box, organizing the electrical wiring, and then connecting it to the tiny house.

———

BUT SHORTLY AFTER Patrick went back to work in 2017 following an awesome few weeks of for the holidays, I was reading quietly at home when there was a knock on the door. It was a debt collector. He claimed that we had failed to pay our loan on the trailer and his company was going to repossess our trailer immediately. It felt like a rug had been pulled from under me. I was in a complete panic. He just kept repeating the same ultimatum, "You must leave." It took a fair bit of probing, but I finally got him to tell me the amount needed to make this horrible nightmare go away. The amount owed on the loan was $10,000 New Zealand dollars. He was adamant that he take the trailer away right then and there. He showed no emotion when I told him we would lose everything if he took the tiny house. He didn't care. The only reason he eventually left empty-handed was that he was driving only a small SUV. When I told him the tiny house wasn't coming off the trailer, he realized he needed a bigger vehicle that could tow it away.

So once Patrick came home that night, we discussed our predicament. As you can probably guess, we were dumbfounded that this had happened to us. I told Patrick all the ways I tried to reason with the man. I'd explained that we had purchased the trailer fair and square. We had proof of payment and a receipt, but the debt collection agency didn't care about it at all.

Our error originated from our naive trust in the young man who sold us the trailer. He said the trailer was his, and that he had the right to sell it directly to us. But in our elation to have found an affordable tiny house trailer, we failed to research how debt is handled in New

Zealand. We didn't look into the local laws or investigate checks and proper procedures for purchasing a trailer. It was only after the fact that we learned that according to New Zealand law, unlike in the United States, a loan follows an object, not the person who owes it.

Because the debt collector came on a weekday, we couldn't move the tiny house to our newly prepared property right away. So I called a local friend who lived down the road and asked if we could keep it there for a few days. I wanted to make sure that our tiny house wouldn't be taken away if we could help it. So while the tiny house was hidden a few streets away, I researched rental companies that had trucks capable of towing the tiny house to Dunedin. Unfortunately, all these companies were in Dunedin, so that Friday we drove to Dunedin, picked up the rental truck, drove back to Waimate, and packed up the tiny house. A few hours later, at around three in the morning, we took the tiny house to Waitati and prayed that the debt collector wouldn't find it there.

The evening that we moved the tiny house was another long night fraught with nerves and anxious butterflies. It was also the first time Patrick and I were in the cab of the truck together while towing the tiny house. There was no cat howling in her crate and no one watching the back of the tiny house sway each time an 18-wheeler passed, but the silence and tense atmosphere made for an exhausting time. It's hard to run on pure adrenaline for four hours. The rental truck managed to tow the tiny house just fine on the flat sections of the highway; however, as soon as the Kilmog (a large hilly area outside Dunedin that State Highway 1 winds through) came into view and the road started getting steeper, the truck began to struggle. Then after a few minutes, the truck stopped working at all.

So there we were. Our only illumination was the weak yellow light inside the truck. Patrick was trying to calm me and prevent me from having a heart attack. The truck had stalled, the tiny house was about to roll back down one of the largest hills among the Kilmog, and the truck's emergency brake was struggling to keep it all together. We didn't even have a chance to pull over, not that there was anywhere to pull over anyway, so we were just in the middle of the highway. Thank god there was at least a passing lane. It was 5:00 a.m. at that point—no garage was open, no one could tow us, and the rental company was still closed.

Patrick, as usual, was cool as a cucumber and just told me the truck was a wee bit tired and needed a rest. So we sat there for about fifteen minutes, letting everything cool down and checking the tiny house, all the while the hazard lights protecting us from the zooming 18-wheelers bombing past us going one hundred kilometers per hour (sixty-two miles per hour). Eventually, the truck started up again, and we crept up the rest of the highway and made it to the property without any further issues.

Patrick's project in Glenavy hadn't quite concluded at that point, so that meant leaving behind the tiny house after we stashed it in Waitati and heading back to Waimate. We lived in the rental accommodation for another two long months without the tiny house. We went back and forth to check on it, work on the plumbing, and to sort out transforming an empty lot to a place that could sustain us and the tiny house. And from a distance, I arranged for water tanks to be delivered, initiated the rural delivery, and got the power to a builder board.

Once we knew the tiny house was safe, we finally had the bandwidth to examine all of our options. We got plenty of advice offline as well. We called two lawyers, my mother, and a police detective. The advice varied wildly (pay the money or take him to court), so we started with the cheapest option: taking the person who sold us the trailer to small claims court.

While we were filling out the form, we learned that we would have to attempt to contact the person first. I did my best to track him down on Facebook, but in the end, we had to hire a private investigator to find him, which cost about $200 New Zealand dollars ($154 US dollars). All that work just to be ignored, which was to be expected. A dirty double-crosser wouldn't be likely to confess on Facebook. So we followed through with the claim, initially asking him to just pay us the money, but it turns out the courts had to give him a chance to make it right himself. After two months of stress and hearings, we got the young man to go to the loan company and transfer the security for the loan from our trailer to his car. Turns out he made a calculated decision to *not* pay off the loan after he got our $3,000 but instead moved to Auckland and hoped that no one would be the wiser.

All in all, the small claims court process was done and dusted in less than six months. Between the first knock on the door and the conclusion of this terrifying episode, there were a whole lot of sleepless nights and stress that could have been avoided if we had known that New Zealand has a pretty unique way of dealing with debt. We know this isn't a common problem everywhere, but it shows that sometimes there are issues that you won't ever see coming.

9

DOWN TO DUNEDIN

 "The people are Scotch. They stopped here on their way from home to heaven thinking they had arrived."

—MARK TWAIN REFERRING TO DUNEDIN, NEW ZEALAND

AFTER SETTLING on the property in Waitati and concluding our unexpected legal situation, we finally felt at peace. It felt like the tiny house had come home. We made progress on the property, finally clearing the most persistent weeds, improving the accessibility, and mitigating the mud. Patrick's new job was a natural progression for him in terms of his career. He was fortunate in securing his new position, and as a result, has worked with some amazing people. It took me a few months to find employment, but once I did, we felt as if everything was finally settled.

I was unsure where to end this story of the ups and downs of our tiny house adventure because as long as we own the tiny house, I won't consider our journey to be over. It truly feels like a part of our family. It was our home from November 2015 until November 2020. For all its crazy, exciting, and challenging years, I wouldn't change that adventure for anything. I feel so thankful that we had the freedom to build our tiny house, the privilege to move it to various locations, and the fortune that my parents let us park the tiny house on their land.

From the first weekends of preparing the tiny house trailer to the weekends spent clearing the property where it rests now, the whole process has been a source of never-ending discovery for Patrick and me. If anything, the South Island Tiny House has taught us that there is no problem we can't overcome. No situation is so dire that we can't push through. From our relationship and coping with the stress and trials of moving abroad to practical issues of troubleshooting our house when our batteries died, it was all part of the process.

Now that we have completed and moved into our more normal-sized home, I feel that we have started a new chapter with the South Island Tiny House. But I relish each opportunity I have to go back up to the tiny house and just relax, put on a record, and start the fire. We are lucky that we can take a step back in time to our young adulthood and can use those memories to help propel us into our next adventure.

AFTERWORD

Join my mailing list to get notified about the next book in this series that continues with our story living in the tiny house in Dunedin!

https://bit.ly/39mRIMW

Thanks for reading.

I would really appreciate it if you could take the time to write a review, it takes a few minutes and helps other readers like you find my book!

ACKNOWLEDGMENTS

Edited by Jillian Harvey.

Proofread and formatted by Armadillo Proofreading.

ABOUT THE AUTHOR

Corianne Holmes is a graduate of Wellesley College. She enjoys brewing homemade wine with foraged fruit, playing with her cat, and reading. This is her first book.

Printed in Great Britain
by Amazon